Foreword by the Joint Chairmen of the Appea

The Rt Hon. Sir Anthony May, Inner Temple
Michael Blair, QC, Middle Temple

This publication celebrates and renders thanks for the restoration, completed in early 2013, of the magnificent organ in the Temple Church to which we have attributed, without apology, John Milton's paean in praise of another organ as 'full consort to the angelic symphony'.

It tells of music and organs in the Church since the early 14th century; of organists who have played the organs and directed the choirs; of the destruction in May 1941 of the famous Father Smith organ of 1680; and of the subsequent most generous gift of the present organ, built in 1927 for a Scottish baronial home.

Installed here in 1954, Lord Glentanar's organ required, nearly 60 years later, a once-in-a-lifetime complete restoration. This it has now received at the hands of Harrison & Harrison, the organ builders of Durham who built it originally, installed it in the Temple Church, and by their skill and expert voicing have in this refurbishment – as was not possible in the straitened 1950s – suited its sound perfectly to the building. The organ now has once more the cohesive and blended sound for which Harrison's instruments are famous. The organ has not simply been repaired; it has been restored to its original and proper glory.

We give heartfelt thanks to all those people and institutions who, by hugely generous financial contributions or other efforts, have paid for the restoration.

Exterior, from Church Court. The Round Church was in use by 1162; the Chancel was consecrated in 1240 in the presence of the King.

Ring out, ye crystal spheres,
Once bless our human ears
(If ye have power to touch our senses so),
And let your silver chime
Move in melodious time,
And let the bass of Heaven's
deep organ blow,
And with your ninefold harmony
Make up full consort to th'angelic
symphony.

John Milton (1608-74), On the Morning
of Christ's Nativity, 125-32

Glen Tanar House, Deeside. The Church's present organ was made for Lord Glentanar, 1923–7, for the ballroom of Glen Tanar House.

Chancel of the Temple Church.

Our committee, appointed by Inner Temple and Middle Temple in 2009, was set the task of raising £750,000, the sum then estimated for the project. Four years later, £750,000 has indeed turned out to be the final cost of the restoration and we are grateful, and indeed delighted, that that sum has been fully contributed.

We have received over 450 individual contributions both large and small. Most have been in money with gift aid; but there has also been welcome generosity in other ways which has led indirectly, but just as valuably, to swell the fund. Notable among this outstanding generosity has been quite spectacular support from almost 300 Benchers of Inner Temple and Middle Temple.

This foreword stands as a warm and sincere expression of our gratitude to each contributor. Our thanks also go to the other members of the committee, and in particular to Penny Jonas, who has responded magnificently to the challenge of administering the appeal and its fund. And we mention with gratitude the additional help given by the two Inns of Court, who have defrayed the full cost of administration, and have thus ensured that every pound contributed by others has gone in full to pay for the restoration.

Temple Church Organ

James Vivian, Organist and Director of Music
Robin Griffith-Jones, Master of the Temple

Wondrous Machine

Henry Purcell, England's greatest composer, whose own music was first published and sold in the porch of the Temple's Round Church in the 1680s, composed a famous piece in praise of an organ: 'Wondrous machine!' This booklet tells of music in the Temple Church over seven centuries and more; of that music today; and of the Church's wondrous organ, now (in 2013) wondrously restored.

The previous organ, as famous in its day as the present instrument, had been built by Father Smith in the 1680s. That organ was played for the last time by a former chorister of the Church on the evening of 10 May 1941. Two hours later, at 11 p.m., the sirens sounded.

The night was clear; the moon was almost full. The River Thames was at low ebb; water pressure was weak. The air-raid – of nearly 100,000 incendiary bombs – lasted all night. A bomb landed next to the parapet at the Church's north-east corner; the fire spread along the roof to the organ, whose woodwork caught fire. One man on fire-watch duty went into the Church and returned with his jacket covered with tiny globules of silvery lead from organ pipes that had melted in the heat. 'At two o'clock in the morning,' a warden recorded, the Temple 'was as light as day. Charred papers and embers were flying through the air, bombs and shrapnel all around. It was an awe-inspiring sight.' By the night's end the Church was a shell; its famous organ, over 250

London Metropolitan Archives

After the bomb, May 1941: the damaged Chancel seen from the Round Church.

The warriors of England, c.1941: montage of service-men and women from the Templars to World War Two, imagined in the damaged Round.

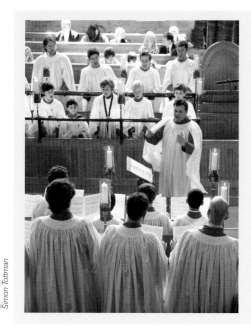

But let my due feet never fail,
To walk the studious cloysters pale,
And love the high embowed roof,
With antick pillars massy proof,
And storied windows richly dight,
Casting a dimm religious light.
There let the pealing organ blow,
To the full voiced quire below,
In service high, and anthems cleer,
As may with sweetnes, through mine ear,
Dissolve me into extasies,
And bring all Heav'n before mine eyes.

John Milton (1608-74), Il Penseroso, *155-66, set to music by Gabriel Jackson for the rededication of the Temple Church Organ, 7 May 2013. The anthem was commissioned by the Temple Music Trust.*

years old, had been destroyed. The night of 10 May 1941 was the worst in London's Blitz; it was also the last. Hitler had already decided to attack the Soviet Union on 22 June 1941, exactly one year after the fall of France. His bombers were heading to the east; they would never return.

Dr George Thalben-Ball wrote, 'The damage to the dear place is quite heart-breaking. That organ can never be replaced, but I hope that something lovely will eventually come in its stead.' We shall read in the following pages just how lovely an instrument was, thanks to the generosity of Lord Glentanar, installed here within fifteen years.

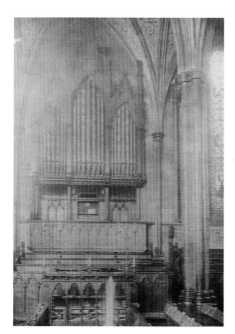

Father Smith's organ of the 1680s, after its move in 1840 to the Chancel.

The organ of the Temple Church, 2011.

The Temple, 1308:

'In the Great Church. Two pair of organs, 40s.'

The Temple Church, built by the Knights Templar, is among the oldest and most beautiful churches in London. The Round Church, in use by the 1160s, was the first Gothic building in England; it was consecrated in 1185. It was modelled on the circular Church of the Holy Sepulchre in Jerusalem, the most sacred place of the Holy Land and so of the whole world.

   The Temple was at the heart of English political life in the Middle Ages. King John relied heavily on the Templars and on their Master, Aymeric de St Maur, for loans and for a safe headquarters on the edge of the City of London but free from the City's control. From the Temple the King issued the charter in November 1214 that guaranteed the freedom of the English Church. A deputation from the barons met the King here, 6 January 1215, for a tempestuous meeting at which they demanded the confirmation of laws and liberties granted by Henry I. The King was back here at Eastertide in April, and again in May when his officials issued from the Temple the charter for London that guaranteed the authority and liberty that the City and Mayor enjoy to this day.

   Aymeric's close friend was William the Marshal, Earl of Pembroke (d.1219), the greatest knight of his age. The Marshal mediated in the negotiations that led to Magna Carta and on 15 June 1215 was a witness at Runnymede. The Marshal was buried, 1219, in our Round Church; his effigy is still here. Among the witnesses to the Magna Carta was Aymeric, who died within a few days of the Marshal and was buried next to him. Among the surety-barons to Magna Carta was the Marshal's eldest son William, whose effigy lies beside his father's in the Round.

   The Church's first, small, chancel was replaced, 1236-40, by the present 'Hall Church' chancel in soaring Early English Gothic style; it was designed to be (but did not become) the burial place of Henry III.

Simon Tottman

Jubilant in Songs of Praise
The Choir and Organs of the Temple Church, 1308

The Templars tended to follow the liturgical usage of their churches' local diocese; Londoners would have found no surprises in the services of the Temple Church.

The Inventory of 1308 reveals much about the Templars' music here. In the Choir a full complement of books was clearly on hand. The antiphoners would have been chant-books for the Office hours, the graduals for the Mass. The tropers would probably have contained Kyrie, Sanctus and Agnus Dei melodies with the addition of trope verses (such as *Kyrie Fons bonitatis* or *Orbis factor*) and very likely the Gloria melody with trope verses *Spiritus et alme orphanorum* as well. Many such tropers also contain a set of sequences (like *Laetabundus* and *Victime paschali laudes*) to be sung after the Alleluia on high feast days; or the sequences could have been copied in the graduals.

In the Church of St Mary were seven more tropers, which suggests that the Marian services were particularly well furnished with music. They may have included polyphonic music too; there is plenty of evidence for singing polyphony at the daily Mary Mass at this period in England. No less than nine processionals were listed; whereas antiphoners and graduals were usually shared, each choir member would have his own processional book, a practical necessity for singing on the move.

In the Great Church were two pairs of organs. ('Pair' indicates a double rank of pipes, so the reference is to two instruments.) At this price and with this disposition we should probably imagine small positive organs of about three octaves range (needing someone to work the bellows). Such organs were quite common in a choir or Lady Chapel, or placed on the rood screen if the screen were strong enough to support the instrument. We read of 'Two cushions to chanters' chairs [one on each side of a divided choir?], and one book for the organs'. The book probably contained the chants where the organ, participating in the performance, elaborated the plainchant, perhaps taking alternate sections.

A breviary has survived of the Templars' services in 'The Temple of the Lord' itself (The Dome of the Rock) on the Temple Mount, the Order's headquarters in Jerusalem. According to the book's dedication-hymns, the faithful must sing to the Lord with harp, pipes and trumpet; the heavenly Jerusalem, realised on earth in the Church's sanctity, is 'full of melody and jubilant in her songs of praise'.

We are very grateful to Professor David Hiley for his help with these paragraphs on the music.

An organist and other musicians accompany King David and his psaltery. Illustration from *The Psalter of St Elisabeth of Hungary*, 1200-17.

Choirmen and choristers singing at a music-stand before an altar. Illustration from a 14th-century Veronese manuscript of *Tacuinum Sanitatis (The Notebook of Health)*.

The Knights Templar were suppressed in 1310. By the late 14th century the lawyers of Inner and Middle Temple were occupying the land and buildings of the Temple. In 1608 their occupancy was secured by the grant of Letters Patent from King James I. The two Inns of Court were granted the land on condition that 'they will well and sufficiently maintain and keep up the aforesaid Church, Chancel and Belfry of the same … for the celebration of divine service and the sacraments and sacramentals and other the ministerial offices and ecclesiastical rites whatsoever henceforth for ever as is befitting and heretofore accustomed.' They have done so, proudly and with generosity, ever since.

Excerpts from the Inventory of the Temple, November 1308, by the Sheriffs of London

In the Great Church.
Six pairs of vestments, with tunics and dalmatics, price of all 48 shillings.
One vestment for festivals, without tunic and dalmatic, 3s.
Five carpets lying before the high altar, and two choir copes, ½ mark.
Two pairs of organs, 40s.

In the Choir.
Five antiphoners [a book containing all anthems and services said or sung in the choir, except the lessons], 3 marks.
Four psalters, 6s.
Four graduals [a book of hymns and prayers, so called because some of the anthems were sung on the steps, *gradus*, of the altar], 20s.
Two cushions to chanters' chairs, and one book for the organs, 5s.

In the Vestry.

Eleven chasubles or Mass vestments of divers colours, 20 marks.

Twenty-eight choir copes, and four little copes for the choristers, price of all, £10.

Two cedar staves [music-stands] for the chanters, ½ mark.

Inner Temple Records, 1519: Order for a Roll to be made containing the names of members of the Society, in order that from them may be raised 70s. for new organs in the church, for the part of the Inner Temple.

Records of the Temple Church, before 1540: The manner of divine Services in the Church, and their charges thereunto … The Festival days they have Mattins and Mass solemnly sung; and during the Mattins singing, they have three Masses said.

April 1554: a requirement for the Treasurer of Inner Temple: to provide books for the singing in the Choir jointly with the Middle Inn.

November 1557: an order issued in both Inns for the assessment of members, for the wages of the singing men for the coming year: In the Middle Temple 12d. from every Bencher and 4d. from other members of the House; and in the Inner Temple 20d. from Knights, 12d. from Benchers, and 4d. at least from every fellow under the Bench, every term.

The Battle of the Organs

The Temple Church only narrowly escaped destruction in the Great Fire of 1666. The Round was scorched, the buildings immediately to the east and south were burnt down. In the 1680s the Inns refurbished their Church in classical style under the direction of the greatest architect of the day, Christopher Wren, whose first marriage had in 1669 been celebrated in the Church. The Inns agreed on the installation of a

new organ, but not which organ-builder to use. In February 1683 the Treasurers commissioned an organ from each of the two leading organ-builders of the time: Bernhard Smith (1630-1708) was Middle's candidate and Renatus Harris (1652-1708) was Inner's. The organs were to be installed in the halls of the Middle and Inner Temple where they were to be played and judged. However, Smith successfully petitioned the Treasurers to install his organ in the Church instead, on a screen dividing the Round from the Chancel. The advantage was short-lived. Harris obtained approval to place his organ at the opposite end of the Church, on the south side of the communion table.

London Metropolitan Archives

View eastwards across the Round, 1805. The back of the organ is above the central doorway into the Chancel.

Father Smith's organ was installed at the west end of the Chancel, 1687-8, on the screen and wall built by Christopher Wren to separate the Chancel and the Round.

Chris Christodoulou

The TEMPLE ORGAN, in its original position, on the SCREEN.

But oh! what art can teach,
What human voice can reach,
The sacred organ's praise?
Notes inspiring holy love,
Notes that wing their heavenly ways
To mend the choirs above.

Orpheus could lead the savage race;
And trees uprooted left their place,
Sequacious of the lyre.
But bright Cecilia raised the wonder higher;
When to her organ vocal breath was given,
An angel heard,
And straight appeared,
Mistaking earth for heaven.

*John Dryden (1631-1700), A Song for
St Cecilia's Day, November 22, 1687,
set to music by George Frideric Handel
(1685-1759), Stanzas VI-VII.*

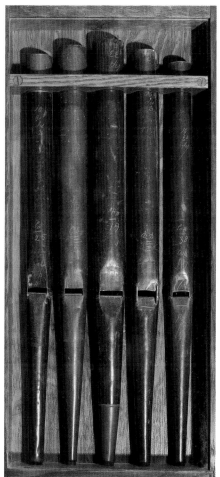

. *M.ᵗˢ Stanley, Organist.*

The finest organists were engaged to show off the instruments. The candidates were put to great expense as the competition intensified and the instruments became more elaborate. The Honourable Roger North, Treasurer of Middle Temple in 1684, was apparently told 'that the partisans for each candidate, in the fury of their zeal, proceeded to the most mischievous and unwarrantable acts of hostilities; and that, in the night preceding the last trial of the reed stops, the friends of Harris cut the bellows of Smith's organ in such a manner that when the time came for playing upon it no wind could be conveyed into the windchest.'

The contest was brought to a close in 1688 when Judge Jeffreys, formerly of Inner Temple, judiciously decided in favour of Middle's candidate, Smith. The price, for not the largest of instruments, was the considerable sum of £1,000. (It did include, however, 'the curtaine rods and curtaines'!). In spite

John Stanley, Organist to Inner Temple, 1734–86. Stanley, blinded at the age of two, became a child prodigy. He was a friend of Handel, and in the 1770s revived Handel's own practice of annual performances of *Messiah* for the benefit of the Foundling Hospital.

Of these five pipes, all except the second are probably from Father Smith's organ. Although subjected in the intervening centuries to re-scaling, shortening, cutting and nicking, they still bear markings typical of Smith.

Father Smith's agreement, 25 May 1688, to maintain for the next seven years the organ he had built for the Church, for a salary of £20 per annum. On the same day Francis Pigott was retained as Organist for seven years.

of defeat, Harris's reputation was greatly enhanced; he used the materials from his Temple organ in instruments made for St Andrew's, Holborn and Christ Church Cathedral, Dublin.

Smith's instrument at the Temple was the first three-manual organ in England and incorporated the newest trends in organ building, such as the 'quarter notes' which enabled the organ to play in keys which – thanks to the tuning system – had previously been undesirable.

The Inns and their organ attracted some of the most famous players in England. Francis Pigott remained in post as Organist here when he was appointed Organist of the Chapel Royal in 1697.

In 1734 the blind prodigy John Stanley was appointed Organist to Inner Temple when he was only 21; he remained in post for 52 years, for the last few of which he was also Master of the King's Band. It was not uncommon for forty or fifty organists – including Handel – to be gathered in the Church to hear him play.

The West Porch: a stationer's advertisement, late 17th century. John Playford, Henry Purcell's first publisher, was clerk of the Temple Church and had his shop in this porch.

Among the most striking names – if not now the most famous – on this board celebrating our Organists is that of Emily Dowding, Organist to Middle Temple, 1796–1814.

Chris Christodoulou

ORGANISTS OF THE TEMPLE

1688 Francis Pigott
1704 John Pigott

INNER TEMPLE	MIDDLE TEMPLE
1729 Obadiah Shuttleworth	1729 John Pigott
1734 John Stanley	1737 James Vincent
1786 Richard John Samuel Stevens	1749 John Jones
1810 George Price	1796 Emily Dowding

1814 George Price
1826 George Warne
1843 Edward John Hopkins
1898 Henry Walford Davies Kt
1923 George Thomas Thalben-Ball Kt
1982 John Anthony Birch
1997 Stephen David Layton
2004 James Antony Vivian
2004 Stephen David Layton
Director of Music
2006 James Antony Vivian
Director of Music and Organist

Donors to The Temple Church Organ Appeal 2011–13

* = Bencher of Inner or Middle Temple   † = Member or Associate of the Appeal Committee

Roderick Abbott

The Lady Ackner's Estate

The Lord Ackner's * Estate

Her Honour Judge Claudia Ackner *

Advocacy Training Council

The Rt Hon. Sir Richard Aikens *

Sir Robert Akenhead *

Allchurches Trust

Robin Allen QC *

Allen & Overy

Brian Altman QC *

Piero and Henrietta Amodio †

Her Honour Shirley Anwyl QC *

The Rt Hon. The Lord Armstrong of Ilminster *

Sir Richard Arnold *

His Honour Judge Sir Gavyn Arthur *

Nicholas Asprey *

Nicholas Bacon and family

Barbara Bailey

Dr Simon Bailey

Sir Philip Bailhache *

The Hon. Justice Baragwanath KNZM QC *

His Honour Judge Brian Barker QC

David Barker QC *

Stephanie Barwise QC *

Benjamin Bather

Andrew and Sarah Baughan

Thomas Baxendale *

Sir David Bean *

Naona Beecher-Moore and Andrew Hobson

Peter Beesley

The Hon. Justice Salihu Moddibo Alfa Belgore *

Sir Rodger Bell *

Sir Christopher Benson *

Guy Beringer QC *† and Margaret Beringer

His Honour Judge John Bevan QC * and Veronica Bevan

Her Honour Christian Bevington *

Stephen Bickford-Smith *

Sir Michael Birt

Elizabeth Blackburn QC *

Alan and Shirley Blair

Magnus, Nina and Campbell Blair

Michael Blair QC *† and Halldóra Blair

David Blunt QC *

Sir David Bodey *

His Honour Judge Guy Boney QC *

Dame Margaret Booth DBE *

Mark Bostock

Anthony Boswood QC *

The Lady Brandon of Oakwood

Janice Brennan *

The Rt Hon. The Lord Brittan of Spennithorne QC *

The J & M Britton Trust, Mr and Mrs Robert Bernays

Stanley Brodie QC *

The Rt Hon. Sir Henry Brooke *

Christopher Brougham QC *

Helen, Lady Broughton

His Honour Judge Mark Brown *

The Rt Hon. Sir Stephen Brown GBE *

Michael Bruce

Adrian Brunner QC *

Adrian Buchanan

Friends of Buckinghamshire Churches

Barbara Bunker

The Rt Hon. The Lord Butler of Brockwell KG GCB CVO *

The Rt Hon. The Baroness Butler-Sloss of Marsh Green GBE *

His Honour Neil Butter CBE QC *

Sir Neil Butterfield *

The Rt Hon. Sir Dennis Byron *

Lady Calcutt

Barbara Calvert QC *

Sir David Calvert-Smith *

Sheila Cameron CBE QC *

Hamish and Anthea Cameron

Godfrey Carey QC *

Lord Carlile of Berriew QC

Hugh Carlisle QC *

The Rt Hon. The Lord Carnwath of Notting Hill *

Sue Carr QC *

Philip Carraro

Sir Edward Cazalet *

The Rt Hon. Sir John Chadwick *

The Chartres Family *

Nicholas Choustikov

The Rt Hon. The Lord Clarke of Stone-cum-Ebony *

Sir Christopher Clarke *

Sir David Clarke *

Liz and Mike Clarke

Mrs T A Clarke

Clerks to Her Majesty's Judges

His Honour Gerald Clifton *

Lady Clothier

Mr and Mrs Piers Clough

Sir Stephen Cobb *

Terence Coghlan QC *

Edward Cole QC

His Honour Judge Nicholas Coleman *

Russell Coleman SC *

Michael Collard

Miss Lynda Collins

His Honour Christopher Compston * and Caroline Compston

Sir Michael Connell *

His Honour Judge Jeremy Connor *

His Honour Peter Cowell *

Mrs Patricia Cox *

Mr and Mrs P Craven

Sir Frederick Crawford *

Dr Stephen Cretney *

His Honour Judge Christopher Critchlow *

Paul Crook

Helen Crosbie

1 Crown Office Row Chambers
His Honour Judge Donald Cryan *
Michael Crystal QC *
The Rt Hon. The Lord Cullen of
    Whitekirk KT *
A J Cunnington
Sir Richard Curtis *
Andrew Dalton
Sheilagh Davies *
Julia Dias QC *
James Dingemans QC *
Kristine Dixon
Diana Dollery
Ian Dove QC *
The Rt Hon. Sir Robin Dunn *
The Rt Hon. Lord Dyson *
Simon Eckersley
Roger Ellis
Michael Elsom
Michael Essayan QC *
Sir Edward Evans-Lombe *
Simon and Luci Eyers
Members of Falcon Chambers
The Rt Hon. The Lord Falconer of
    Thoroton QC *
Richard Farnhill
The Rt Hon. Sir Donald
    Farquharson *
Mrs Brenda Farthing
Mr Justice Nial Fennelly *
Richard Fernyhough QC *
Guy Fetherstonhaugh QC *
Sir Richard Field *
Her Honour Judge Elisabeth
    Fisher *
Michael Fitzgerald OBE QC *
Charles Flint QC *
Sir Christopher Floyd *
Jacqueline Flurscheim
The Hon. Tan Sri Dato' James
    Foong Cheng Yuen *
Sir Thayne Forbes *
His Honour Giles Forrester *
Mr and Mrs Frank Frame
Robert Francis QC *
Jill Franklin and Bob Allies
Freshfields Bruckhaus Derringer
Friends of Cathedral Music
The Rt Hon. Sir William Gage *
John Gardiner QC *
Sir Patrick Garland *

Mr Justice Hugh Geoghegan *
Charles George QC *
Charles Gibson QC *
Nigel Giffin QC *
Annie Gladwell
Dame Elizabeth Gloster DBE *
Golden Bottle Trust
Jeff Golden
Professor Sir Roy Goode CBE QC *
Michael and Pat Goodman
His Honour Judge Gerald Gordon *
James Goudie QC *
His Honour John Gower QC *
Mrs J M Grant
Professor Malcolm Grant CBE *
The Lady Grantchester
George and Grace Gray Trust
The Reverend Robin Griffith-Jones
    *†
The Rt Hon. The Lord Griffiths MC *
Jeffrey Gruder QC *
Field Marshal the Lord Guthrie of
    Craigiebank *
Anthony Hacking QC *
The Rt Hon. Dame Heather Hallett
    DBE *
Mr and Mrs A W Hamilton
The Rt Hon. Lord Hamilton *
Alastair Hammerton *
Mrs C C Harding
Rosina Hare QC *
Professor Carol Harlow QC *
His Honour Judge Charles Harris
    QC *
Sir Michael and Lady Harrison
His Honour Judge Sir Mark
    Havelock-Allan QC *
Philip Havers QC *
His Honour Richard Havery QC *
Roger Henderson QC *
Memorial service for The Rt Hon.
    Sir Denis Henry
Dame Rosalyn Higgins DBE *
Professor Mark Hill QC *
Elizabeth Hindmarsh
Memorial service for The Rt Hon.
    Sir David Hirst
Jonathan Hirst QC *
The Lady Hobhouse of
    Woodborough
Sir Christopher Holland *

Sheila Hollis *
Daniel Hollis QC *
The Rt Hon. Sir Anthony Hooper *
    and Lady Hooper
His Honour Judge Toby Hooper
    QC *
John Hopkins *
Stephen and Charmian Horan
Rosamund Horwood Smart QC *
    and Richard Bernays
The Rt Hon. The Lord Howe of
    Aberavon CH QC *
Gideon Hudson
His Honour Judge Iain Hughes
    QC *
His Honour John Hull QC *
David C Humphreys
Archie Hunter
Saran Morgan Hutchins
The Rt Hon. Sir Michael Hutchison
Brian Hutton
The Rt Hon. The Lord Hutton *
Ben Hytner QC *
Nigel Inglis-Jones QC *
Joint Inns Residents' Association
Anthony Isaacs MBE and Jenny
    Isaacs
J.B. and K.I.L. Izatt
Sir Raymond Jack *
Donald Jackson
Peter Jackson
Sir Peter Jackson *
The Rt Hon. Sir Rupert Jackson *
Sir Martin Jacomb *
Anita James *
The Hon. Daniel Janner QC *
Jaymount Investments
Sir Brian Jenkins GBE *
Robert and Philippa John
Sir Robert Johnson
Lady Johnston
Penny Jonas *†
His Honour Judge Nicholas Jones
Derek Jones
The Rt Hon. The Lord Judge of
    Draycote *
Steven Kay QC *
Keating Chambers
Colleen Keck
The Rt Hon. Sir David Keene *
Lady Kilner Brown

Charles Kimberley

Dr Adam Kimberley

The Rt Hon. The Lord Kingsdown KG *

Her Honour Frances Kirkham CBE *

Sir Andrew Kirkwood *

Tyrone Landau

Sir Gordon Langley *

Roddy Langmuir

The Rt Hon. Sir John Laws *

Lady Laws

Lady Patricia Layfield

Valentine Le Grice

Sir Godfray Le Quesne QC *

Simon Lee

Sir Thomas Legg KBE QC *

Sir George Leggatt *

Alison Levitt QC *

Sir Sydney Lipworth QC *

Richard Lissack QC *

Brigadier Peter Little CBE *

Miss Jane Lloyd

His Honour Humphrey LLoyd QC *

The Rt. Hon. Sir David Lloyd Jones * and Lady Lloyd Jones

The Rt Hon. The Lord Lloyd of Berwick *

Stephen Lloyd *

The Rt Hon. Sir Andrew Longmore * and Lady Longmore

Dorian Lovell-Pank QC *

Her Honour Judge Caroline Ludlow

The Rt Hon. The Lord Mackay of Clashfern KT *

Patrick Maddams †, in memory of Geoffrey Charles Maddams

Sir David Maddison *

Richard Mair

Sir Stephen Males *

Baroness Mallalieu QC *

Guy Mansfield QC *

John Marrin QC *

Roy Martin QC *

Stephen Mason

Lady May

The Rt Hon. Sir Anthony May *† and Lady May

Her Honour Judge Juliet May QC *

Ian Mayes QC *

The Rt Hon. The Lord Mayhew of Twysden QC *

Sir Charles McCullough *

Glenys McDonald MBE

Kristine McGlothlin †

Don McGowan

The Hon. Justice John McGrath *

Harvey McGregor QC *

The Hon. Michael McLaren QC *

The Reverend and Mrs Hugh Mead

Simon Medland QC

David Melville QC *

Iain Milligan QC *

Hannah and Elina Mistry

His Honour E F Monier-Williams *

The Rt Hon. Sir Martin Moore-Bick * and Lady Moore-Bick

Christopher Morcom QC * and Diane Morcom

Marilynne Morgan CB *

David Morgan

Sir Michael Morland *

Guy Morton

His Eminence Cardinal Cormac Murphy-O'Connor *

Edward Murray

Junka Nakata and Andrew Sulston

William F Neburagho

The Rt Hon. Sir Brian Neill *

Catherine Newman QC *

Sir George Newman *

Helena Newman for Max Todes and family

Lauretta Newman

The Rt Hon. The Lord Nicholls of Birkenhead *

Sir Peter North CBE QC *

Edward Nugee QC *

Christopher Nugee QC *

Sir James Nursaw KCB QC * and Lady Nursaw

Sir John Nutting QC *

The Oldhurst Trust, HMJ Ritchie

Professor Dawn Oliver QC *

Sir Stephen Oliver QC *

Sir Peter Openshaw *

His Honour Denis Orde * and Miss Georgina Orde

European Chapter of the American Guild of Organists

David H O Owen

Joanna Page

His Honour David Paget QC *

Dr Roy Palmer

Jackie Palmer

Anthony Papadimitriou *

Mervyn Parry

Nigel Pascoe QC *

Sir David Penry-Davey *

Mr and Mrs Brian Pickard

Roger & Ingrid Pilkington Charitable Trust

David Pittaway QC *

Mrs Audrey Platz in memory of Kenneth Martin Platz

His Honour Judge Timothy Pontius *

John Powell QC *

Michael Pratt QC *

Richard Price OBE QC

Leolin Price CBE QC *

Edwin Prince *

Andrew Pugh QC *

The Rt Hon. Dame Anne Rafferty DBE

Anthony Ratcliffe MBE

Rev. Canon John Rees

Robert Rhodes QC *

His Honour Michael Rich QC *

The Rt Hon. The Lord Richard of Ammanford QC *

His Honour Judge Jeremy Richardson QC *

The Rt Hon. Sir Bernard Rix *

His Honour Jeremy Roberts QC *

Mrs Anne Robinson

Mrs Christopher Robinson

Christopher Robinson Trust

Vivian Robinson QC *

Dr Frank Robson

Martin Rodger QC

Thomas Roe and Helen Berry

Guy Roots QC *

Graham Rose

The Rt Hon. Sir Christopher Rose *

The Lady Roskill

Alison Ross

John Rowe QC *

Imogen Rumbold

The Rushworth Charitable Trust

Haidje Rustau

Gerard Ryan QC *

Paul and Susan Ryan

Timothy Saloman QC *

Richard Salter QC * and Ginnie Salter
Deborah Saxby
Michael Sayers QC *
Mrs E Y Scandling
The Rt Hon. Sir Konrad Schiemann *
Peter Scott QC *
The Rt Hon. Sir Scott Baker *
Robert Seabrook QC *
Oliver Sells QC *
Caroline Shea
Lady Sheen
The Rt Hon. Sir John Sheil *
Lady Sheldon
W Richard Siberry QC *
Ben Simms
Robin Simpson QC *
Dame Elizabeth Slade DBE *
Jonathan Small QC
Nigel P Smith
Joe Smouha QC *
Mrs Brenda Somerset-Jones
Michael Soole QC *
Richard Southwell QC *
Professor John Spencer QC *
Andrew Spink QC *† and Susan Spink
George Staple CB QC *
The Rt Hon. Sir Christopher Staughton *
D W Stevens
Mrs Mary Stevens
His Honour James Stewart QC *
Rodney Stewart Smith *
His Honour Eric Stockdale *
His Honour Gregory Stone QC *
Jeremy Storey QC *
The Rt Hon. Jack Straw MP *
Miss E Studley

Her Honour Judge Linda Sullivan QC *
David D H Sullivan QC *
Mark Sutherland
Peter Sutherland KCMG SC *
Dame Caroline Swift DBE *
Christopher Symons QC *
Andrew Tait QC *
Robert-Jan Temmink and Caroline Gill
Temple Music Foundation
Temple Music Trust
Anthony Temple QC *
Inner Temple
Middle Temple
Victor Temple QC *
The Rt Hon. The Lord Templeman *
Mark Tennant *
Roger Ter Haar QC *
His Honour Judge Peter Testar
Dame Kate Thirlwall DBE *
Michael Thomas CMG QC *
The Rt Hon. Sir Swinton Thomas *
Simon Thorley QC *
His Honour Judge Roger Thorn QC *
Jonathan Thornton
Professor John Tiley CBE QC *
Henrietta Newman for Max Todes and family
The Rt Hon. Sir Stephen Tomlinson *
Keith Topley *
The Toulmin Family
His Honour John Toulmin CMG QC *
Mrs Georgina Trevelyan-Clark
Sir Michael Tugendhat *
Henry Turcan *
Sir Michael Turner *
James Turner QC *

Professor Dame Margaret Turner-Warwick DBE *
His Honour Judge David Tyzack QC *
Mrs B D Vara
David Vaughan CBE QC *
Ghislane Weder Veludakis
Robert Venables QC *
Nicholas Vineall QC
James Vivian and Ann Elise Smoot
Sir Timothy Walker *
LCH Clearnet Ltd in memory Susan Ward *
Sir Nicholas Warren *
Weaver's Company Benevolent Fund
Robert Webb QC *
Dame Gillian Weir DBE *
Christian Wells
Garfield Weston
David Whitehead
The Most Rev and Rt Hon. Dr Rowan Williams *
Stephen Williamson QC *
Tony Willis
The Rt Hon. The Lord Wilson of Culworth *
The Wolfson Foundation
International Association of Women Judges
Mr and Mrs A Woodthorpe
The Rt Hon. The Lord Woolf of Barnes *
Anna Woolley
Michael Worsley QC *
Brigadier Charles Wright *
Mr and Mrs Malcolm Wright
David Wurtzel *
David Yale FBA QC *
Benedict Zucchi

We are also most grateful to those generous donors who wish to remain anonymous and to all those who contributed to the Church's many collections in support of the Appeal. We acknowledge too with warmest thanks the support of Dame Gillian Weir DBE, Crispian Steele-Perkins and Ian le Grice, who gave recitals in support of the appeal; Donald Jackson; Liz Clarke and all who helped organise or who supported the Church's Fairs and Fetes; and the Dunwich Dynamo Cycle Riders and their many sponsors. There may also be some unattributed donations received after the final printing date for this publication.

Foundation of the Modern Choir

By the 1820s it was clear that the Church needed structural repair; this was commissioned from Robert Smirke in 1826. Fashion had changed; Smirke proudly revived, where he could, the Church's Gothic character. With this work still ongoing, the Inns appointed two professional singers to perform at services. By the 1830s two women and two men were employed to sing from the organ loft above the entrance to the Round. 'The curtain,' we are told, 'would be drawn aside for a few minutes, the singers would sing, and everybody would turn west to look at them; then the curtain was banged to with a rattle of brass rings.'

By now the Inns were ready for the full-scale Gothic refurbishment of the Church. In 1840 the organ-screen was taken down and the Round and Chancel were re-unified. The organ was moved to its present position on the Chancel's north wall. To match the building's renewed splendour, the Inns agreed to the temporary appointment of a small choir of men and boys. The organ too was enlarged; the first pedal stop

The organ after the move to its present position in 1840.

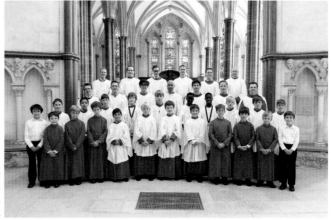

Dr Edward John Hopkins, Organist of the Temple Church, 1843-98, and Director of the Choir from 1869. Hopkins is still remembered as the father of modern Anglican psalmody.

The Temple Church Choir, Walford Davies seated in the centre.

Simon Tottman

The Temple Church Choir, 2012.

was 'so tremendous in its effect that it used to shake the spectacles on the noses of the Benchers'.

In 1843-4 the Inns confirmed the choir's establishment, moved it to new prominence on either side of the Chancel in alignment with the organ, and appointed as organist Edward James Hopkins. Hopkins would be in post for 55 years; he became famous as the father of Anglican psalmody, writing dozens of the chants for the Book of Common Prayer that have been in use ever since. Not everyone was pleased by these developments. The Master complained about the choir's ever-expanding role: he was often not in the pulpit to start his sermon until one o'clock. Some things at least have changed.

But some things remain the same. Under Hopkins' direction the music of the Temple Church – its organ and its choir – became as famous as any church music in London. Over a century after his death, that renown is as secure and well-deserved as it has ever been.

Hopkins was followed here by Sir Henry Walford Davies (organist, 1898-1923), who in 1919 selected the young George Thalben-Ball as Acting Organist. In 1923 Thalben-Ball took over as Organist; and so began a new era of extraordinary distinction. Most famous of all the recordings made here under his direction was the first. In 1927 the choir recorded Mendelssohn's *Hear My Prayer* with the Temple chorister Ernest Lough

In the practice room: Walford Davies and the Choir.

as the soloist. Within six months, the original master of this recording had worn out; a replacement, the version still available today, was made a year later. Over six million copies have been sold. For two years after its release the crowds attending Sunday service in the Temple were such that admission tickets were introduced. Thalben-Ball, who became renowned worldwide, retired in 1982 after 59 years in office and was, shortly afterwards, knighted.

Sir George Thalben-Ball, Acting Organist of the Temple Church from 1919, Organist 1923-81.

Six Dixon brothers served as Temple Church choristers from 1900 to 1919: Alfred Capel Dixon, Walter Howard Dixon, Charles William Dixon, Harry Sydney Dixon, Horace Uttey Dixon and George R. Septimus Dixon. Walter Howard Dixon (1891-1915) and Harry Sydney 'Squib' Dixon (1897-1915) were both killed at Ypres; they were the first of the Temple's former choristers to be killed on active service in World War One. In the course of our Organ Appeal, we have been touched by the generosity of many people; no gift has been more moving than those of two sisters, great-nieces of the Dixon brothers, who contributed in the memory of the two who were killed.

A Phoenix from the Ashes

Over the course of 250 years the Smith organ – like organs in many other ancient churches and cathedrals – became larger and more complex in line with organ-building developments and with the tastes of the organ loft's incumbents. By 1941 the organ reflected the need for an eclectic instrument that could both accompany increasingly complex liturgical music and perform a wide concert repertoire. Marion Scott (1877-1953), the friend of Ivor Gurney and champion of his music, knew the Temple Church well before World War Two. She particularly loved the tones of its organ which, she said, 'stood to other organs in the same relation as a perfect Stradivarius to other violins', making it 'almost as sensitive as a string quartet'.

In the late 1940s Dr George Thalben-Ball, Organist of the Temple Church and doyen of English choirmasters, was among those supervising the Church's repair after the war. Both Harrison & Harrison and Walker's had such full order books that the Temple would have to wait for at least five years.

Dr Thalben-Ball had played and admired the organ at Glen Tanar before the war. It was a large and beautiful Harrison & Harrison, built in 1927 in the great tradition of English romantic organs. By chance, Thalben-Ball met Lord Glentanar again after the war, in Cambridge, and asked after the organ. Lord Glentanar regretted that it was under-used; indeed, if Dr Thalben-Ball could suggest a good home for it Lord Glentanar would willingly offer it, as a gift, to a new owner.

Marcel Dupré, 1886-1971, composer and organist, with Lord Glentanar.

Marcel Dupré at the keyboard of the Glen Tanar organ. Dupré played the organ at its inaugural concert, 1927.

Thalben-Ball could suggest, with great gratitude, the best of all possible homes: the Temple Church. The organ's move took months of work; and on 23 March 1954, at the rededication of the Chancel by the Archbishop of Canterbury in the presence of the Queen Mother, the glorious Glen Tanar organ was heard in the Temple Church for the first time.

Lord Glentanar's gift of the organ was conditional on its installation here by Harrison & Harrison. (It has been in the care of Harrison's ever since.) 'This offer fills me with delight,' Thalben-Ball wrote. 'The organ, a four-manual "vintage" Harrison instrument, is probably better than anything that could be obtained new at the present time, and in many respects equals, and in a few surpasses, the old Temple organ.'

The Glen Tanar organ arrived in London by train on 6 July 1953. A generous organ chamber 33ft wide, 18ft deep and 40ft high was built on the north side of the church, where the previous organ had been located, to house the instrument. The organ occupies two bays: the western bay contains the Tuba, Great Reeds and the Choir and Solo Organs, the eastern bay the Great and Swell Organs. The Pedal pipes are split between the two. Lord Glentanar wished that the organ should not be altered without his permission: 'Its balance is well-nigh perfect and any additions would need to be very carefully considered and very beautifully executed.' In fact the only change to the specification was the addition of the Double Ophicleide 32ft in the pedal which gave the full organ greater depth.

The organ has, since the refurbishment of 2011–13, 66 stops, the size of instrument usually found in an English cathedral. Its longest pipes, which provide the deepest bass frequencies, are 32 feet long while the smallest pipes in the treble registers are only a few inches in length. Each pipe (the organ now has 3,828) has been skilfully crafted and 'voiced', and relies on a complicated mechanism to transfer the player's intentions from the keyboard. It is unsurprising that until the onset of the Industrial Revolution the pipe organ was the most complicated machine encountered in everyday life.

Her Majesty The Queen, Her Majesty The Queen Mother and His Royal Highness The Duke of Edinburgh at the Temple Church, 7 November 1958, for the rededication of the Round Church after its post-war repair.

Her Majesty The Queen and His Royal Highness The Duke of Edinburgh at the Temple Church, 24 June 2008, at the 400th Anniversary of the Letters Patent to the two Inns.

The Creation and Installation of the Organ at Glen Tanar House, 1923–7

The Temple Church organ was built for Lord Glentanar. Here are some excerpts from the archives of the organ-builders, Messrs Harrison & Harrison, who made the organ, then moved it to the Temple in the 1950s, and refurbished it, piece by piece, in 2011-13. At Glen Tanar, the instrument occupied a large chamber behind the ballroom's stage, underneath which lay the 32ft pipes of the Double Open Wood. In front of the stage was an orchestra pit. Arthur Harrison, in charge of the voicing, overcame the subdued acoustic with characteristic style.

From Lord Glentanar to Messrs Harrison & Harrison Ltd, Organ-Builders, Durham

28 April 1923

Dear Sirs

I have for some time past been contemplating building an organ here and am considering certain structural alterations to my ballroom for this purpose. Before definitely deciding on this I would like to have the opinion of a practical organ-builder as to whether my proposals would give correct and sufficient space for the type of organ I wish to install.

I would therefore be glad if you could arrange to send a representative of your firm to meet me here at an early date. I shall be in residence until 9th May.

Yours faithfully

Glentanar

From Lord Glentanar to Arthur Harrison Esq, Organ-Builder, Durham

13 October 1923

Dear Mr Harrison

I have been thinking a lot about the specification of my organ recently. As you know, the one thing I want to be sure about is above all things a grand and majestic ensemble, and when you are considering the scale of the pipes, if you are ever in doubt as to whether it should be a little smaller or a little larger in scale, please choose the latter. I would much sooner have you err on the big side than on the other.

Yours very faithfully

Glentanar

3 September 1927
Inaugural Performance of Lord Glentanar's new organ: Newspaper Report

Lord Glentanar invited his neighbours on Saturday to assist in the opening of the new organ which he has installed in Glen Tanar House. Lord Glentanar's devotion to music and his taste and liberality where it is concerned are matters of common knowledge, and his guests on Saturday were no doubt prepared for something quite different from the usual inauguration recital. Nor were they disappointed.

The new organ stands in a chamber which has been specially built for it at the end of the Ballroom of Glen Tanar House, a spacious apartment with a lofty, antler-studded roof. Together with a power, greater perhaps than may be fully used with comfort to the listener, the organ has a remarkable range and variety of effect disclosed to the best advantage by the masterful playing of M. Marcel Dupré.

Lord Glentanar conducted the choir and orchestra in a Purcell chorus and in *Die Meistersinger* overture and showed himself no less expert in this as in other executive branches of the Art. He has a vigorous and vivid style.

This organ is both a beautiful, versatile solo instrument and a perfect accompaniment to the Church's choir and liturgy. Here its ability to provide subtle nuance and a wide variety of tonal colours is invaluable. The Harrison instrument and the choir complement each other perfectly and they have very much become – through many recordings, concerts and broadcasts – the Temple 'sound'.

The organ is still very much a 1920s 'Imperial' instrument at heart. The Great Organ has a smooth and well developed diapason chorus capped by two reeds; the Solo Organ has the very 'keen' family of strings, powerful high-pressure Tuba and imitative voices such as the French Horn and Orchestral Hautboy (an old term for Oboe); and the Choir Organ has the delicate flutes and some additional imitative voices. The console was renovated in 2000 and is of the typical Harrison design: curved key cheeks and 'golf-tee' pistons. It is a most elegant piece of furniture as well as being immensely comfortable to play.

Minor tonal changes by Thalben-Ball and Dr John Birch were made in the decades after its installation that have enabled the instrument to give a good account of compositions from many different periods. A well-established series of free Wednesday lunchtime organ recitals demonstrates this versatility.

The 2013 rebuild has enabled the Temple organists and Harrison's to reassess the tonal balance of the instrument. Andrew Scott Head Voicer of Harrison's, who had already cared for the organ for over a decade with immense dedication and

Called to the Bar: Inner Temple's students are called to the Bar in the Church, here in the presence of Master HRH The Princess Royal, Royal Bencher of the Inn.

HRH Prince William at Choral Evensong in the Church prior to his call to the Bench of Middle Temple, 2009.

skill, has with his colleagues sought to preserve the organ's original accent without diminishing its versatility. A view was taken that any additions should be in the original style, and as a result the pipe metal and scales of the new stops match the existing 1920s pipe work. Four new stops have been added to the Great Organ: a 4ft Principal, a 2ft Fifteenth, a 1 3/5ft Seventeeth and a Mixture of three ranks. These stops create a secondary unenclosed chorus from 16 ft through to Mixture which can then be transferred to the choir manual and used in dialogue with the main chorus of the Great Organ. The Mixture of the Choir Organ has meanwhile been returned to its original designs. A full specification of the restored 2013 instrument is reproduced at the end of this booklet.

Phil Ripley

Angelic Symphony

In the last twenty-five years, the music of the Church has been under the direction of Dr John Birch, Stephen Layton and the present Organist and Director of Music, James Vivian, whose Assistant Organist since 2006 has been Greg Morris. Four Organists have had good reason to be grateful to Ian le Grice, who came to the Church as a boy-chorister in 1957 and finally retired as Associate Organist in 2012.

The choir's recent schedule has included tours, broadcasts and concerts. The choir has premiered new works by composers such as Thomas Adès. In 2003 the choir performed the overnight premières of Sir John Tavener's massive work *The Veil of the Temple* at the Temple Church itself, and in 2004 took *The Veil's* full version to the Lincoln Center Festival in New York and an abbreviated version to the BBC Proms in the Albert Hall. The choir's CD of *The Veil* has been followed by its *The Majesty of thy Glory* and *A Festival of Psalms* CDs, both on the Signum Classics label and both received with great critical acclaim.

Seven hundred years after the Sheriffs of London listed the two pairs of organs and the choirmen's and choristers' copes in the Temple Church, our organ, choirmen and choristers continue to make music worthy of this beautiful Church, to the glory of God and to the

Dr John Birch, Organist of the Temple Church, 1982-97.

James Vivian, Organist and Director of Music of the Temple Church, 2006-present.

Stephen Layton, Organist (and then Director of Music) of the Temple Church, 1997-2006.

Simon Tottman

delight of all those who hear them in the Church itself, in our broadcasts and in our recordings. At the heart of it all is the 'wondrous machine' that has now been restored to its pristine splendour.

Wedding of Michael Haswell and Joanne Kerr

Soul of the world!
– so Purcell addresses music in his Ode to St Cecilia –
Thou tun'st this World below, the Spheres above,
Who in the Heavenly Round to their own Music move.
With that sublime Celestial Lay
Can any Earthly Sounds compare?
If any Earthly Music dare,
The noble Organ may.

Wondrous machine!

Simon Tottman

Restoring the Temple Organ

Mark Venning, Chairman, Harrison & Harrison

The English Romantic organ reached its zenith in the period between the two World Wars. Harrison & Harrison were known as its leading exponents, and the Temple Church organ is a classic example. It is characterised by a rich variety of orchestral and accompanimental voices, splendidly complete choruses, and voicing that reached a matchless level of refinement. No less impressive is the standard of craftsmanship and technical design.

Thus the Temple organ's unusual history has undoubtedly affected its sound. Built in 1927 for Lord Glentanar and entombed behind the stage of the ballroom in his Scottish mansion, a room which was 'as dead as it well could be', it was transplanted 26 years later to surroundings that could hardly be more different. The Temple Church provided a generous organ chamber with good tonal projection in a beneficial acoustic. The success of this transition stands as a remarkable achievement. We can be sure that the organ now sounds more forthright than it did in its original home – but it is no less eloquent for that.

Hitherto the organ contained no fewer than 3,474 pipes, ranging in length from 32 feet to the size of a pencil; their number has now been increased to 3,828. The restoration of this masterpiece is a correspondingly complex and demanding operation. A team of four organ-builders from Harrison & Harrison dismantled the organ

Before the restoration: the Great Organ.

James Vivian

James Vivian

After the restoration: new and old pipes of the Great Second Division.

New pipes of the Great Second Division.

in August 2011; much of the pipework was stored in the gallery of the Round Church (a grand staircase being specially constructed for that purpose), to be cleaned in situ by our London staff. All other working parts of the organ, including the reed stops, were brought back to our workshop in Durham. Now work could begin in earnest.

First and foremost, our aim has been to preserve the organ's musical character. All the pipes have been cleaned individually: in ancient times they were washed in beer, a custom which the organ builders doubtless appreciated, but today we just use soapy water. The reed pipes have to be dismantled for cleaning of the delicate tongues and shallots. Then, after the organ has been re-assembled, our voicers have the task of re-creating the proper speech and balance of the whole organ. This delicate work involves much the same creative process as when the organ was first built. In other words, we must step into the shoes of Arthur Harrison and apply the same musical criteria – bearing in mind that the organ has been translated from its original home, and that the sound has been subtly modified over the years by dirt and other external factors. For six weeks or more, our voicers checked and regulated each pipe, working in the church to rebuild the tonal architecture of the whole organ – a fascinating process demanding great concentration, though a tedious experience for the casual listener. Our intention has been that the organ would once again sound as A.H. intended. Without losing sight of this overriding aim, a few changes have been carefully planned in consultation with the Director of Music, James Vivian, in order to increase its versatility; details can be seen in the stop list on this publication's back cover.

The organ's mechanism and wind system are integral to its character and had likewise to be meticulously restored. This practical side of the work is in some ways more straightforward, though no less exacting. With all the working parts returned to the workshop after some 85 years, we have had a rare opportunity to evaluate the original craftsmanship at close quarters, and our team of some 40 craftsmen and apprentices has made every effort to do it justice.

The wind chests (complex wooden structures which supply the wind to each individual pipe) had been affected by low humidity caused by the church's central heating. All have been fully restored, a painstaking process involving many pints of animal glue, many hundreds of screws, and many weeks of craftsmen's time. Ten of the thirteen wind reservoirs, or bellows, have been releathered. The intricate electro-pneumatic